M000158669

BOOSTING *Your Pet's* SELF-ESTEEM

or How to Have a

Self-Actualized,

Addiction-Free,

Non–co-dependent

Animal Companion

MICHAEL JAMES DOWLING

Illustrations by Sarah Buell Dowling

DISCARD

 Howell Book House
New York

Copyright © 1997 by Under the Lamb, Inc. Text by Michael James Dowling
Illustrations by Sarah Buell Dowling

All rights reserved. No part of this book may be reproduced or transmitted in any
form or by any means, electronic or mechanical, including photocopying,
recording, or by any information storage and retrieval system without permission in
writing from the Publisher.

Howell Book House
A Simon & Schuster Macmillan Company
1633 Broadway
New York, NY 10019.

MACMILLAN is a registered trademark of Macmillan, Inc.

ISBN: 0-87605-680-X
Library of Congress Cataloging-in-Publication Information available upon request.

Manufactured in the United States of America
99 98 97 10 9 8 7 6 5 4 4 3 2

Designed by George Mckeon

#14.95

NOV 9 '10

BOOSTING Your Pet's SELF-ESTEEM

DISCARD

To Sadie, Rufus, Millie, Pee-Pees, and Tangy for your support and inspiration. Your lives are proof that the principles espoused in this book really work.

Table of Contents

About the Author and Illustrator

*M*ichael James Dowling has written and lectured extensively on pet self-esteem. He has contributed numerous articles to *Pet Psychology Today* magazine, and is the author of several best selling books, including *How to Keep From Losing Your Self-Esteem While Your Domestic Companion Is Raising His* and *The Effect of Perpetual Nudity on Self-Esteem.*

Sarah Buell Dowling graduated from the Multicultural College of Art with a degree in gender-equity cartooning. She likes animals. This is her first book.

Preface

I am aware that this book may cause considerable controversy. Self-esteem is a sensitive subject, especially when it pertains to one's significant others. We must remember, however, that no progress is made without risk. Therefore, I will fearlessly persevere in the quest for a better world, leaving fate to decide my place in history.

The reader may be interested to know how the author chose to deal with the cumbersome limitations of our patriarchal legacy, the English language. Obviously, I wanted to avoid the male chauvinistic or radical feministic solutions of putting all pronouns in the masculine or feminine forms, respectively. And to use both the masculine and feminine forms (i.e., he/she or s/he) on every occasion would be unwieldy.

Therefore, I decided to use unisex software on an androgynous computer to randomly generate male and female pronouns. The danger, of course, was that this might result in some confusing sentences (e.g. " . . . his self-esteem was so low that she . . . "), but confusion is a small price to pay for equality and fairness.

Michael Dowling
Charlottesville, Virginia

Part 1

The Crisis

THE IMPORTANCE OF HIGH SELF-ESTEEM

What you are about to read may shock you. The revelations disclosed in this book are probably new to you because hitherto the government, in a conspiracy with the liberal left and the radical right, has attempted to suppress them. The time has now come to unleash the truth if our world is to evolve to a higher level of consciousness.

For the past decade I led a team of eminent pet psychologists in a top secret research study funded by the N.I.A.H. (National Institute of Animal Health). Our findings conclusively show that millions of our nation's pets are not living up to their full animal potential because they suffer from low self-esteem.

How your pet feels about himself crucially affects every aspect of his behavior. Pets with good self-concepts form more genuinely meaningful relationships. They make better choices when faced with life's important decisions, such as where to bury a bone, or whether to use the kitty litter or the backyard. In general, they climb higher on the ladder of success.

On the other hand, pets with low self-esteem don't even know there is a ladder of success. They tend to have limited vocabularies and even more limited world views. They act out problems instead of working them out. Of course, you don't want your pet to live a life like that!

The fact that you are reading this book indicates that you care about your pet's well-beingness. You are to be affirmed for consciously choosing to ascertain whether or not your pet has a poor self-image, and if so, how you can help him break the cycle of self-defeating behaviors and realize the inner confidence that is the by-product of self-celebration. I commend you. I want to help you because I like you. So, let's embark on our adventuresome journey of self-discovery together, shall we?

SOME SYMPTOMS OF LOW SELF-ESTEEM

Perhaps you naively believe that the majority of pets have healthy self-images. You may even think most pet behaviors seem pretty normal. But appearances are deceiving. The tragic truth is that because pet low self-esteem is so wide-spread, we have come to regard many pet behaviors as normal when actually they are neurotic.

Not long ago my dog, Percy, and I visited a friend, whom I shall call John. John had several pets. He adored them and often showed me photos of them. I was eagerly looking forward to meeting John's pets, and was glad that they all happened to be home when I arrived. Imagine my shock when I saw that every one of them exhibited symptoms of low self-esteem.

John's dog immediately came over to us, wagging his tail and sending indirect signals that he would like to be petted. He obviously had a deep need for approval that manifested itself in people-pleasing behavior. To make matters worse, he was anal-compulsive around Percy.

John pointed out how contented his cat was as she slept on the chair, purring loudly. For fear of damaging John's self-esteem, I couldn't bring myself to tell him that his cat's behavior didn't indicate contentedness, but depression. She was using sleep as an escape mechanism to avoid the pain of living with a poor self-image. She wasn't purring. She was bemoaning her fate in life.

Over in the corner of the room, John's fish was barely coping with life as he struggled to keep his head above water. His boa was constricted and uptight. And John's parakeet was eating dinner alone, her claws tightly clutching the perch. She looked tight-lipped and tense, and just pecked at her food.

Perhaps this single incident will help you to appreciate how widespread the problem of pet low self-esteem is. The symptoms are so common, we think they indicate normal behavior.

How about your pets? Does your dog have a compulsive need to be liked, which manifests itself in a life-controlling addiction to being petted? Does your cat have an addiction to apathy; so laid back she can't be upfront? Is your boa a pain in the neck? Does your fish just float there, staring out into water? If so, I've got disturbing news for you. They're dysfunctional.

A dysfunctional boa is a pain in the neck.

CONFRONTING THE CRISIS

At this point, if you are a typical pet owner, you are probably trying to deny there is a problem. "Not my pets," you say. "And look at Lassie, Rin Tin Tin, Garfield, Pavlov's dog, and Cleopatra's cat. Did they have low self-esteem?"

But your denial is simply the first stage of the grieving process as you come to grips with the enormity of the crisis. Don't look to those few famous pets for answers—they're part of the problem. The media sets up unrealistic expectations by glamorizing impossible role models, further damaging your own pets' self-esteem.

So don't deny and repress, decide and redress. It is up to you to choose to do the work necessary to help your pets. Remember, no pain, no gain. Don't be guilty of minimization or rationalization, choose actualization.

If you are a bit frightened at this point, I understand. But remember, I am here to help you. You can trust me.

You can trust me.

Do you recall my friend, John? You will be encouraged to know that I was able to treat his dog, cat, boa, parakeet and fish with the therapies I will discuss in the following pages. Now his pets have said "yes" to their beingness and are fully functional. With my help, you can do the same for your pets.

In the next section of this book I will give you some encouraging examples of how I have used cutting-edge therapy to help pets overcome some major neuroses. Succeeding chapters will tell you how you can help your pets in your own home. Finally, we'll talk about some long-range solutions that will make our society and our world a more supportive environment for pets to be their essential selves.

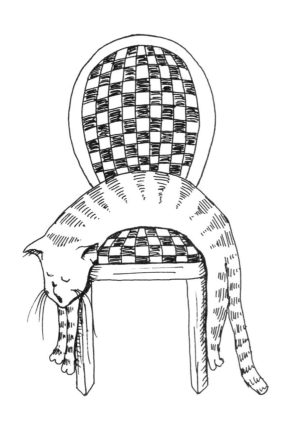

Part 2

Low Self-Esteem Pathologies and Treatments

ATTENTION DEFICIENCY DILEMMA

Frank sat across from me in my office with his two dogs, Oscar and Penelope. Penelope seemed lethargic. Her tongue hung out one side of her mouth, and she looked at me with a hangdog expression. Oscar, on the other hand, appeared bright-eyed and alert, and wagged his tail continuously.

"I'm worried about Penelope," admitted Frank, bursting into tears. "She's very, very sweet, but all she does is nap, nap, nap. Occasionally she will crawl to her bowl and lap, lap, lap. She seems unmotivated, enervated, and disconnected. I've tried everything, but she doesn't respond. Can you help us?"

In the caring, professional manner for which I am so much admired, I let Frank know I empathized with his pain. Then I surprised him. I told him it wasn't Penelope he should be concerned about—it was Oscar. "Oscar's tail wagging is a tell-tale symptom of low self-esteem," I said. "Tail wagging is what we psychologists call a 'coping mechanism.' Oscar needs professional help."

Frank wisely agreed to my treatment recommendation. After extensive family systems group therapy with Penelope, Oscar, and Frank, I concluded that Oscar had an attention deficiency dilemma (ADD). It turns out that he came from a large litter, and at a very early age he did not get the attention he needed. As a result, he developed insecurities about whether or not he was accepted for who he was. He compensated as an adult by seeking the approval of others through neurotic attention-getting behaviors, such as tail wagging.

Fortunately, through massage therapy, I was able to help Oscar get in touch with his puppy within. Today Oscar is free from his addiction to self-defeating happiness behaviors. He has a well adjusted personality and is living authentically. Frank, I might add, is still in therapy and progressing nicely.

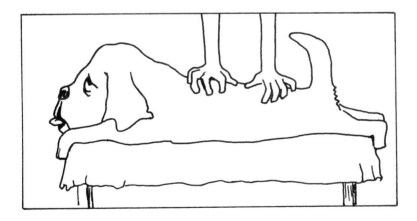

Massage therapy helped Oscar get in touch with his puppy within.

Because ADD is such a common malady for dogs, I will cite one more example from my confidential files. As I was counselling Ralph and Hugo in my office, Ralph suddenly exhibited a neurotic symptom. "Has he always barked?" I asked.

Hugo was proud of Ralph's barking, and actually encouraged it. "He's a wonderful watchdog," he said.

Hugo seemed surprised when I told him that Ralph's barking was a symptom of low self-esteem. "Ralph is emotionally immature and is trying to get attention in inappropriate ways," I explained. Fortunately, Hugo agreed to enter Ralph in therapy with me.

Over the next few months I successfully treated Ralph's attention deficiency dilemma through a combination of rolfing and repolarizing. Today Ralph no longer barks, even when Hugo's house was recently robbed.

The discovery that barking is a symptom of low self-esteem was a scientific break through. For years pet psychologists had wondered why small dogs tend to bark more than large dogs. Now we know it's because vertically disadvantaged dogs have enormous self-esteem issues to deal with.

CATATONIA

The dictionary defines *catatonia* as "a schizophrenic disorder characterized by plastic immobility of the limbs, stupor, negativism, and mutism." It is obvious from the name that catatonia is particularly common in cats. But only recently was it discovered that this disorder stems from a poor self-image.

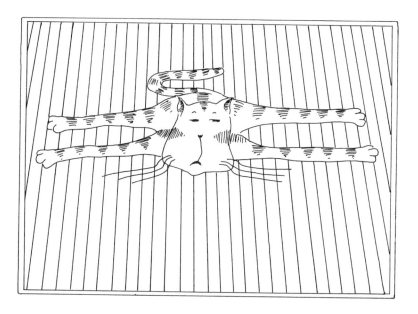

Cats with poor self-images have different coping mechanisms from dogs. They don't wag their tails to appear happy, or bark to call attention to themselves. Instead, they cope by acting aloof, as if they couldn't care less what anyone else thinks. Cats in advanced stages of catatonia are often interactionally schizophrenic, asking for affection one minute and withdrawing in cool aloofness the next.

Harriet came to see me one day with her cat, Henry. "He's indecisive. He can't make up his mind whether he'd rather be inside or outside," she complained. "I spend half my day opening doors for him." As Harriet talked, Henry sat on her lap, looking defensive.

"Cats with a poor sense of self-worth only appear to be indecisive," I explained gently to avoid hurting Harriet's self-esteem. "Actually, they have such a poor self-image they're trying to get away from themselves. That's why they want to go outside when they're inside, and vice versa. But Henry's indecisiveness also could be catatonia. Let's give him a few tests to be sure."

The tests revealed that Henry not only was catatonic and had low self-esteem, but he was also passive-aggressive. Instead of expressing his upsetness in appropriate ways, he delighted in manipulating others into co-dependent behaviors, such as opening doors for him.

Once this negative passive-aggressive behavior pattern was identified, Harriet and Henry nullified their co-dependency neurosis and were able to make more in-tentionally fulfilling co-relational lifestyle choices. Unfortunately, one of the lifestyle choices Harriet made was to kick Harry out of the house, but I am confident Harry is now living more authentically wherever he is.

*Cats with poor self-images don't like being with themselves. They
spend a considerable amount of time trying to go
somewhere where they are not.*

PHOBIAS

Many pets with low self-esteem are crippled by fear. A patient I will call Tutweiler, for sake of anonymity, was perhaps my most extreme example of this problem.

When Mary, Tutweiler's owner, brought him into my office, Tutweiler just sat there on my desk, completely withdrawn into his own little shell. I knew immediately from my professional training that he was introverted. "He's very withdrawn in social situations," Mary told me in anguish. "What can I do, Doctor?"

I decided that guided meditation would be the best treatment for Tutweiler. I invited him to shut his eyes, inhale and exhale deeply, and relax his whole body, from the point of his beak to the tip of his tail. As he became more comfortable, I asked Tutweiler to visualize himself in the warm sun with other friendly turtles walking up to him saying wonderfully affirming things, such as "What beautiful beady eyes you have."

For Tutweiler, this meditation was such a powerful experience that he refused to terminate it for eight months. Of course, if you do this meditation with your pet and he doesn't have such a powerful experience, that's okay too.

Mary told me recently that it has been three years since Tutweiler has gone through withdrawal symptoms. He is willing to stick his neck out, and has become much more relationally transparent.

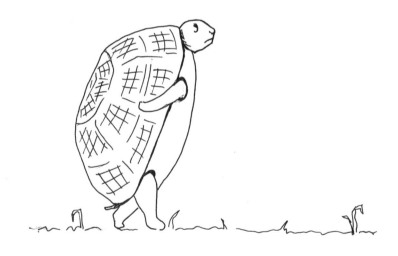

SPECIES IDENTITY ISSUES

Whoever invented the species name "bulldog" would not be very popular at a convention of pet psychologists. Because of this confusing name, bulldogs often suffer from low self-esteem due to species identity ambivalence. On occasion, they may even find cows attractive. Of course, we all know there is no right or wrong about such feelings of attraction. However, when cows don't reciprocate, it can damage the bulldogs' self-esteem.

Species ambivalence syndrome is also very common with catfish, bird dogs, and sheepdogs. Greyhounds, who are not gray, also have problems. Fortunately, species clarification tapes can work wonders with such problems.

29

Mental imaging is excellent for helping pets overcome irrational fears, such as felineophobia.

Meditation will reduce your pets' stress and help them to center.

31

*Assertiveness training will give timid,
listless pets a confidence boost.*

If you overdo the assertiveness training and your pets become hyper-aggressive, help them to compose themselves by enrolling them in sensitivity training.

IMAGE ISSUES

Your pet's image has a tremendous impact on his or her self-esteem. This explains the rising popularity of catacombs.

Cosmetic surgery is becoming increasingly popular to help dogs who are self-conscious about facial hair and hangdog expressions.

Has it been a long time since you saw your bird smile? A class in image and self-projection techniques can give a tense canary a winning personality.

ADDICTIONS

Twelve step programs are popular for treating addictions and boosting self-esteem, but one has to be creative in applying them to pets. For example, it takes dogs, cats, turtles, and other pets with four legs at least 24 steps to show improvement.

It is not uncommon for fish with low self-esteem to drink 24 hours a day. For obvious reasons, fish with drinking problems need 12 stroke programs instead of 12 step programs.

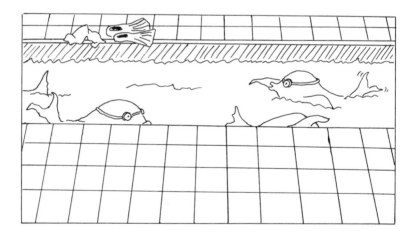

DOMESTICATION REPRESSION

House pets tend to repress their true feelings in order to adjust to a domesticated environment. They let their rational selves overwhelm their emotional selves, so that their inner selves cannot project to their outer selves, inhibiting their Real Selves.

For example, house cats typically have difficulty emoting because they suppress their ancestral links to lions and tigers. Fortunately, primal growl therapy can help an inhibited cat turn a wimpy purr into a healthy roar.

Part 3

Self-Esteem
Begins at Home

I hope the previous examples have given you encouragement that low self-esteem in pets can be remedied. But you don't need to wait until you have enough money to enroll your pets in expensive therapies. Here's how you can start right now—in your own home—to introduce your pets to their authentic selves.

DE-PROGRAMMING NEGATIVE SELF-IMAGES

The first step on the road to recovery is to de-program your pets from their negative self-concepts. Assemble your pets in a friendship circle and gaze lovingly into each other's eyes. Take deep breaths, inhaling and exhaling together in a relaxed, natural manner. Encourage your pets to center by visualizing a happy thought, such as a dog bone or clean kitty litter. Reassure them in a soft voice that high self-esteem is their birthright, and that it is your intention to help empower them to lead more self-actualized lives. Pledge together in unison to stop enabling one another's pathologies, to be here now in the universe, and to eat healthy, all-natural foods.

Gather your pets in a friendship circle and help them to center.

After you have built mutual trust with the friendship circle exercise, I suggest that you have each of your pets keep a daily mood log for one week. Here are sample mood logs for some of my own pets.

My Dog's Mood Log

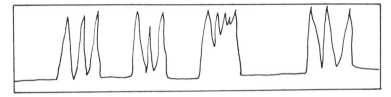

My Cat's Mood Log

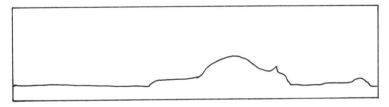

My Fish's Mood Log

AFFIRMATIONS

Once your pets have been de-programmed from negative self-concepts, they need to be re-programmed through cognitive therapy using positive affirmations. For the next exercise, you and your pets should stand in the nude in front of a full-length mirror. Have your pets affirm their bodies just the way they are with positive truth statements such as, "My fins are in," or "My beak is neat," or "My shell is swell."

Remind yourselves that affirming does not have to mean liking, simply accepting. Encourage your pets to give themselves permission to discard negative "should statements," such as "I should have a nicer beak." Discover your "I AMness" by reciting self-actualizing truth statements together, such as the following:

- ◎ I am beginning to love my paws and claws. They are perfect just the way they are.

- ◎ As I breathe deeply, I am experiencing love for my whole self, including my paws and claws.

- ◎ I am clearing my mind of all negative thoughts and experiencing universal love, because I love my paws and claws.

- ◎ My paws and claws are in all ways always getting better and better, and so am I!

At the end of the exercise, pat yourselves affectionately on your cheeks, muzzles, or whatever, look in the mirror, and say out loud, "I like you."

On the next two pages are some more positive affirmations for your dog and cat to recite out loud several times a day.

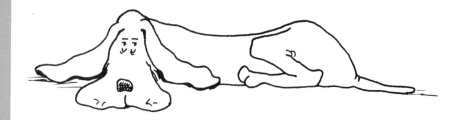

DYNAMIC DOG'S DOGMA

⦾ Nothing is so fine as an actualized canine.

⦾ My bark is not worse than my bite, they're both just right.

⦾ Fleas are attracted to me because of my magnetic personality.

⦾ "God" is simply "dog" spelled backwards.

⦾ Some say this is a dog-eat-dog world.
I say its a dog eat hotdog and steak world.

⦾ I've got the world on a leash.

CONFIDENT CAT'S CATECHISM

◎ You're looking at the magnificat.

◎ Nothing's so sublime as a confident feline.

◎ Real cats don't eat fîche.

◎ I'm not catnapping; I'm visualizing my next life's goals.

◎ I'm for animal rights, and I have a right to wear my fur coat if I want to.

◎ Some say meow, I say me-wow!

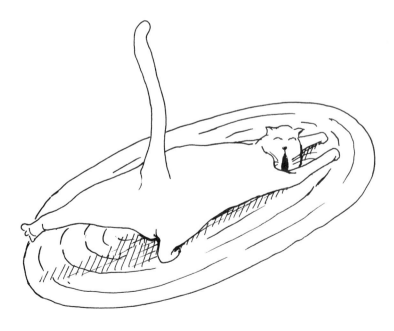

Part 4

Getting to the Core Issue

HUMANARCHIC EXPLOITATION

The exercises above are helpful, but unfortunately they don't address the core issue. The major cause of low self-esteem in pets is the species victimization, inequality, and authoritarian oppression they experience. Pets live in a humanarchy. They are exploited by an unfair eco-socio political system.

For example, do you have a big house while your dog has a little house?

Do you sleep in a warm, comfortable bed and eat at a table while your pets sleep and eat on the floor, or in a cage or in a bowl? If so, no wonder your pets have low self-esteem!

Self-image and multi-species bonding are enhanced when your family sleeps together . . .

. . . and eats together.

Note: This may necessitate some forethought in your menu planning. It is obviously insensitive to serve chicken to your bird.

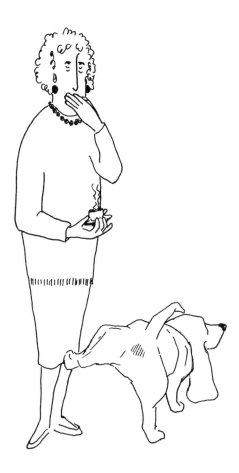

Unhappiness comes from thwarted desires arising from negative injunctions. Never criticize your pets or tell them "No!" This causes them to repress their natural desires and damages their self-esteem.

Leashes are a terrible threat to your pet's self-esteem. Leash laws should be abolished. They discriminate against pets. But, in the meantime, until they are abolished . . .

. . . we recommend that you use an equality leash. It has collars at both ends.

EDUCATION

Another major cause of low self-esteem in pets is illiteracy. Over 99.9% of pets can't read, and that may be just the tip of the iceberg.

Of course, the problem is that the government has spent pathetically little money on pet education over the past 100 years, as the graph below shows:

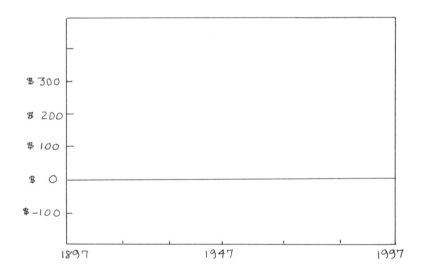

Annual Per Cat Educational Expenditures

Education is key to raising your pets' self-esteem. But don't send your pets to obedience schools, those authoritarian relics of the 1950s, in which tyrannical trainers use derogatory words that damage self-esteem.

Instead, enroll them in multispecies, multicultural educational programs, which will help them appreciate their cultural heritages.

PET OWNERS' SPEECH CODE

Enlightened pet owners must eliminate species-insensitive speech from their vocabularies.

The phrase, "A dog is man's best friend," is an excellent example of speciesist speech. This hurts the self-esteem of dogs because it puts the human in the power position.

A more pro-dog wording would be, "A man is dog's best friend." However, this phrase may hurt the self-esteem of humans.

The more egalitarian expression, "Dog and man are best friends," tends to exclude other species, damaging their self-esteem.

Therefore, I recommend replacing the phrase, "A dog is man's best friend," with, "All species are best friends, and no species are better friends than any others."

"Raining cats and dogs" and "there's more than one way to skin a cat" are obvious examples of inappropriate speech because they connote violence to pets. "Has the cat got your tongue" stereotypes cats as thieves, and words such as "catastrophe" and "cataclysm" unfairly depict cats as the source of major problems. This type of speech should never be used.

Here are some more politically incorrect expressions that are prohibited by the enlightened pet owners' speech code:

Dogmatic

Dog gone

In the dog house

Dog breath

Dog tired

Jail bird

Bird brain

Snake oil

Snaky

Cataplexy

Copy cat

Catapult

Catty

Cataract

Fishy

Fisheye

A fine kettle of fish

Pigheaded (or Guinea
  Pigheaded)

Speciesist speech is rampant throughout our literature. Take the following familiar nursery rhyme as an example:

Old Mother Hubbard

Old Mother Hubbard, went to the cupboard,

To get her poor dog a bone,

But when she came there, the cupboard was bare,

And so the poor dog had none.

This nursery rhyme is offensive to dogs. In the first place, it labels the dog as "poor," which stereotypes him as either economically disadvantaged or as the object of pity, or both. The fact that Mother Hubbard went to the cupboard to get the bone for the dog implies dependency, as if the dog was unable to get the bone for himself.

It is also clear that this dog was the victim of culinary discrimination because someone else had already eaten the meat off the bone. And finally, the story tells us that the dog went without any bone at all, while it is strangely silent about what the elitist Mother Hubbard had for dinner. Probably, she left her dog at home and went out to eat at the kind of restaurant that discriminates against pets.

The previous nursery rhyme is so familiar that you may not have noticed how politically oppressive it is until now. Yet, this is just one example of many I could cite. What do you think we're communicating to our children about equal rights to education while reading to them that it was against the rule for Mary's little lamb to follow her to school one day? We must cross this type of humanarchic literature off our reading lists.

Even the word "pet" is loaded with disparaging, authoritarian, possessive, and speciesist connotations. The deprecatory aspects of the word are obvious, of course, because we all know that "petty" means small, trivial, and insignificant. The more subversively negative characteristics are less obvious until one remembers that the very word "pet" necessarily entails the existence of an owner. Ownership connotes capitalistic possessiveness and speciesist domination. "Owner" and "pet" also imply roles, and roles subjugate beingness.

You should replace the word "pet" with the more acceptable term "domestic companion." This frees you from the role of tyrannical owner so that you can fulfill your true destiny as a benevolent, co-equal domestic companion's companion. Then you and your fellow domestic companions, liberated from the bondage of politically oppressive speech, can enjoy a mutually affirming domestic companionship.

Part 5

Evolving Toward Transformation

TOWARD PERSONAL TRANSFORMATION

*Y*ou and your significant others will increasingly feel confidently up to life's challenges as you harmonize together in a mutually supportive domestic companionship. You will naturally foster each other's self-esteem by consciously choosing to emancipate yourselves from the authoritarian notion of behavior that places the concepts of good and bad outside yourselves. You will express your likes and dislikes as preferences, and will refrain from imposing external standards of right and wrong, knowing that such anti-life injunctions produce guilt and damage self-esteem.

Once you and your domestic companions give yourselves permission to appropriate the realization that there is no right or wrong, your self-esteem will ascend to its maximum potential, unfettered by the rules and constraints that oppress the unenlightened. There will still be struggles, of course, such as when your dog is anal-expletive and poops on your carpet. But in the cosmic sense, such struggles are to be welcomed because they present opportunities for personal growth.

TOWARD SOCIETAL TRANSFORMATION

Boosting the self-esteem of all domestic companions everywhere will require not only a transformation in personal consciousness, but a consciousness-raising transformation in our society as well. The top positions in our government, corporations, and universities must be opened to all species.

This will take concerted political action because today, most government agencies, corporations, and universities won't even let domestic companions into their buildings.

Domestic companions are victims of rampant unemployment. Most live from day to day on handouts. We need to include them in our welfare programs so they can be liberated from the trap of economic dependence.

We must eliminate the discrimination that excludes domestic companions from our healthcare system. So-called "universal coverage" is a sham when most hospitals won't even give a cat a cat scan.

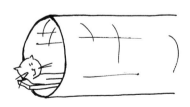

In the enlightened society of the future, health insurance applications will look something like this:

Universal Non-Speciesiest Health Insurance Application Form

Name _____

Address _____

Species* _____ Sex** _____

Age*_____   Number of legs* _____

Color of hair, fur, feathers, scales, or shell*_____

_____

Blood type:* Hot____ Cold_____

We do not discriminate on basis of species, sex, age, number of legs, temperature of blood, or color of hair, fur, feathers, scales, or shell. Therefore, answering these questions is optional.

**If the category "sex" is offensively limiting to you, you may substitute one of the commonly used "genders," or make up one of your own.*

We must fight for justice and equality to bring revolutionary transformation to our society!

Join the Domestic Companion Crusade and—

◎ Develop a mutual empowerment plan with your own domestic companions.

◎ Demonstrate in front of pet stores and kennels that subjugate pets. Boycott restaurants, stores, and hotels that discriminate against pets.

◎ Start a petition drive to abolish leash laws and obedience schools.

◎ Don't speak to people who speak speciesist speech.

◎ Fight to ban speciesist literature from our libraries and bookstores.★

◎ Support an Equal Species Amendment (ESA) to the Constitution.

◎ Write your elected officials (a sample letter is on the next page).

★Of course, I don't advocate banning speciesist literature from our schools. That would be censorship because it would interfere with students' rights to clarify their values regarding speciesism.

Write your elected officials and let them know your views on speciesism. Use the sample letter below.

Sample letter to photocopy, sign and mail.

Dear Mr. President:

I am appalled at the way our nation tramples on the self-esteem of pets. I demand that we outlaw leash laws, abolish discrimination against pets, and make our national bird the parakeet. If you do not act decisively on these issues, my pets and I will join the pet suffrage movement and vote to replace you with a hamster.

Yours truly,

It won't be easy to bring this transformation about. It may take millions of years, but it will be worth the effort. Just imagine how wonderful the world will be when it is full of self-confident, self-actualized, self-realized, self-centered domestic companions!

It will no longer be necessary to pet dogs because they will have overcome their pathological need for approval.

- ◎ Turtles will come out of their shells.

- ◎ Birds won't get their feathers ruffled so easily.

- ◎ Hamsters and gerbils will quit the rat race.

- ◎ Cats will drop their aloofness facades and make worthwhile contributions to society.

- ◎ Leashes, collars, cages, dogcatchers, and obedience schools will be no more.

Oppression will end!

Equality will reign!

*The New Age of the Animal Potential
Movement will dawn.*

Everyone will be happy . . .

... as all around the world holistically healed

domestic companions and domestic companions'

companions evolve together toward higher cosmic

consciousness, holding hands, wings, fins,

hoofs, and claws in peace, love, equality

and universal specieshood!

Bibliography

Arthur, I. Emma. *Fetch It Yourself, An Assertiveness Manual for Dogs.* New York:Random Chance Press, 1996.

Cellar, N. D. *Why Mary's Lamb Can't Read.* New York: Amazing Schoolhouse Books, 1995.

Freeman, Betty. *The Feline Mystique.* New York: The Harbor Bazaar, 1996.

Gates, O. Penn. *Dog Bytes; A Computer Primer for Dogs.* New York: Full Court Press, 1996.

Ibid, I. B. *It's a Great Day for Great Danes: Essays on the Coming Emancipation of Pets.* New York: Airedale Press, 1996.

Jung, Connie. *Animal Lib: An Idea Whose Time Has Come.* New York: Freedom Reigns Books, 1996.

Kessler, Frederick B. *Humanism: An Idea Whose Time Has Passed.* Chicago: Pet Psychology Today, August 1996.

Litter, Kitty. *Going For the Gusto All Nine Times Around.* New York: Beagle Books, 1994.

May, Rollov R. *I'm Bow-Wow, You're Bow-Wow.* New York: Bench Press, 1997.

Marx, Harp O. *The Canine Manifesto.* San Francisco: Universal Equality Publishing, 1995.

Marx, Veronica. *The Feline Antipasto.* San Francisco: Better Books for Better Cooks, Inc., 1996.

Melon, Mac, M.D. *The View from the Dog House.* New York: Proceedings of the Pet Psychology Association Annual Meeting, May 1996, pages 34–67.

Nam, Sue D. *Studies of Tail Wagging, Barking, Purring and Other Symptoms of Low Self-Esteem in Pets.* Washington, D.C.: National Institute of Animal Health Publications, 1997.

Terrapin, Tutweiler T. *How I Learned to Stick My Neck Out and Succeed.* Boston: Reptile Publishing USA, 1996.

Index